Original title:
Footprints in the Frost

Copyright © 2024 Creative Arts Management OÜ
All rights reserved.

Author: Dorian Ashford
ISBN HARDBACK: 978-9916-94-568-1
ISBN PAPERBACK: 978-9916-94-569-8

Pathways Woven in Winter's Embrace

Down the path we squish and slide,
With laughter ringing far and wide.
Oh, look, there's a snowman trying to dance,
He's got two left feet; what a chance!

Every step a slippery jest,
We slip and slide—who's the best?
The dog jumps high, chasing a bird,
While I trip over my absent word.

Softly Gliding Over the Ice

On ice-skates, we glide and sway,
Like penguins playing in disarray.
Watch out for that post; it's a trap,
Johnny just fell with a perfect clap!

Each swirl spins stories, crisp and bright,
While trying to balance feels like flight.
We strike poses, but fall like logs,
As the whole world laughs with the frogs!

Clear Imprints Under the Pale Moon

The moonlight shines on our grand parade,
With every slip, our dignity fades.
I think I'll join the cat in the snow,
She looks so graceful—how does she know?

We glide like stars, then take a dive,
Our winter wonderland feels alive.
But here comes Mom, with her steaming stew,
We're told to have fun, but please no voodoo!

Touched by Winter's Chill

Bundled up tight, oh what a sight,
Trying to run, but it just isn't right.
The cold air bites; we squeal and yell,
As we land in a drift—oh, can't you tell?

With snowballs flying like crazy blimps,
We dodge and weave, avoiding the wimps.
But there's always one with a mischievous spark,
And suddenly I'm buried; it's a snow shark!

Traces of Joy in the Chill

In the morning light, we glide,
With clumsy boots, what a ride!
Snowballs fly, laughter rings,
Frosty art, the joy it brings.

Our noses red, we skip and hop,
In chilly air, we never stop.
Silly pranks and snowmen tall,
Winter's fun, our blissful call.

The Dance of the Winter Wanderer

A twirling jig in the snow so white,
Spinning round till the world feels right.
With every slip, we laugh and cheer,
What a sight, the winter frontier!

A tip here, a tumble there,
It's a frosty dance without a care.
The ground is slick, yet we persist,
In frozen mischief, we can't resist.

Conversations in the Crystal Orchard

In the orchard wrapped in chill,
Snowflakes whisper, hearts they thrill.
Chattering squirrels play hide and seek,
While our cheeks glow, bright and cheek.

With frosty breath, we joke around,
A merry band in winter's gown.
The trees grow quiet, listen close,
As laughter echoes, loud and gross.

Frost-laden Remnants of Time

The cold air bites, but we're all smiles,
Tripping over snowdrifts, adjusting our styles.
Sledding down hills, what a wild ride,
On this winter stage, we laugh with pride.

But wait! A snowball aimed for me,
A friendly duel 'neath the frosty tree.
In the chill, our worries cease,
As we frolic in the snowy fleece.

Ghosts of the Frozen Ground

In winter's chill, they slide and sway,
Frozen spirits at play each day.
They tiptoe 'round on icy toes,
Leaving behind where nobody goes.

Snowmen laugh with carrot noses,
While little penguins strike goofy poses.
Ghostly giggles fill the air,
As frosty pranks unfold with flair.

Memories Woven in White

A snowball fight turns quite absurd,
The cat's attacked, it's feared, not heard.
Sledding races, friends collide,
Wipe out's the score, no need to hide.

We reminisce with icy grins,
Of crazy times and snowy spins.
Who knew a frost could spark such cheer,
With giggles echoing all the year?

Prints of a Wandering Heart

A squirrel dashes, loses its cap,
Leaves funny trails of a silly trap.
A dog dashes by, thinks he's a knight,
Chasing his tail with frosty delight.

As winter bites, the world turns bright,
With laughter dancing in the twilight.
Wandering souls on an icy spree,
Create snowprints for all to see.

Frost-kissed Echoes of the Past

Are those old boots from last year's romp?
Frosted surprises in every clomp.
Chasing each other, we slip and slide,
With frozen giggles we take our ride.

Grandma's sweater, all knit and knotted,
Worn in the fun that fate allotted.
Echoes of laughter crisp with ice,
Frosty footprints; oh, so nice!

Frosty Glimmers in the Soft Light

Tiny crunch under every step,
I slip and slide, oh what a rep!
Frosty glimmers like glassy tricks,
One wrong move, it's a slip and click!

Winter's canvas invites some fun,
With every tumble, the laughter's spun.
Giggling kids leave trails of cheer,
As snowmen form—oh dear, oh dear!

Chilled Echoes Along the Way

Each step sounds like a frosty sneeze,
The chill's a prankster, if you please!
A dance of shivers, we shuffle through,
Watch out for that icy puddle, woo!

Mittens flying, hats take flight,
Sleds are soaring in pure delight.
Chilled echoes ripple in the air,
Laughter lingers, bold, not rare!

The Pathway of Silent Heroes

Braving cold with fingers red,
A quest for snacks, we forge ahead.
Silent heroes, we march in style,
Stomping snow with a cheeky smile!

But who will win the snowball fight?
The competition's fierce tonight!
Snowflakes falling like confetti bold,
Stories carved in white, retold.

Glacial Whispers of the Past

Once upon a time, frost was keen,
Created mischief where we've been.
Glacial whispers swirl and play,
Who built this ramp? Oh, what a display!

The frozen ground has secrets deep,
With jolly echoes that never sleep.
Let's dance around with glee and cheer,
Winters past are always near!

The Path of the Silent Traveler

In winter's chill so crystal bright,
A traveler slips, oh what a sight!
With flailing arms and a comical dance,
They land with grace, or not, perchance.

The snowflakes giggle, the trees they cheer,
As the traveler mutters, 'Oh dear, oh dear!'
Each step a slip, each slip a jest,
In this frosty land, they're quite the guest.

Echoing Hearts through Frozen Realms

With frozen toes and noses red,
The echoes laugh, words left unsaid.
Two hearts collide in a playful shove,
Snowball flights, here's winter love!

They chase each other, around they go,
Sliding and slipping, to and fro.
A heart-shaped mark in the snow soon forms,
Amidst the laughter and winter storms.

Weathered Marks on Winter's Canvas

With each little step, a story unfurls,
Of unsteady legs and frosty twirls.
In the powdery snow, giggles do wake,
A tumble here, a wobbly shake!

Amidst the chill, they forge ahead,
A trail of laughter, as joy is spread.
Every patch tells a tale so bright,
Of merry missteps in the pale moonlight.

Enigmas Beneath the Cold Starlight

Under a blanket of twinkling light,
They tiptoe cautiously, oh what a fright!
A crunch, a squeak, a slip of the shoe,
They chuckle and giggle at what they construe.

A snowman grins with a carrot nose,
Watching the chaos as laughter grows.
Starlit follies, a dance so absurd,
Winter's own comedy hardly deterred.

Chilling Impressions on Winter's Canvas

In winter's chill, a dance we share,
With sliding steps, oh what a flair!
Our boots may trip, but spirits fly,
As laughter rings beneath the sky.

A slip here, a stomp of glee,
Making snow angels, feeling free.
Cocoa warms our laughter bright,
While frost paints our cheeks with delight.

Shadows on a Frozen Trail

Through icy paths, we strut with style,
With wobbly moves that make us smile.
The echoes of our giggles chase,
As we tumble down in frozen grace.

Boots like clowns on a frosty stage,
Each slip a tale, a winter page.
An artful leap, a flurry of fun,
This winter walk has just begun.

Traces of a Winter's Walk

In crunching snow, our tales unfold,
With foot-stomps bold and laughter told.
A snowball flies, a playful shot,
A dance of joy in every plot.

With cheeks aglow, we brave the freeze,
Chasing snowflakes, hearts at ease.
As socks get soaked and antics reign,
We'll make these memories worth the gain.

Paths through the Crystalline Veil

Amidst the sparkles, we dare to roam,
Creating chaos away from home.
With every slip, our worries fade,
In this frosty escapade we've made.

The moon above gives us a wink,
As icy puddles make us think.
We'll slip and slide, yet never quit,
Choosing joy in each frosty bit.

Memories Etched in the Chill

In frosty air, we danced around,
With laughter that could shake the ground.
We painted snowmen, round and tall,
And watched them melt, as a waterball.

A snowball fight, a chilly race,
Socks got wet, what a silly grace!
With every slip, a giggly sound,
Our joy was lost, then quickly found.

A snow angel, we took a leap,
And left behind a frosty heap.
We trotted back, through icy gust,
And sure enough, our boots had rust!

So here's to winters, wild and wise,
With frosty fun under gray skies.
We'll giggle long at all we've tossed,
'Cause in the snow, we never lost!

Threads of Warmth in the Cold

Bundled up in layers thick,
We laughed at how the ice would stick.
Hot cocoa mugs, a marshmallow sky,
We toasted to winter, oh my, oh my!

We slid on ice with little grace,
Each tumble turned into a race.
Laughter echoed, icy and bright,
As we slipped and spun, what a sight!

In snowy coats, we'd stomp around,
Creating chaos, laughter abounds.
Our mittens tossed, in playful fights,
While frost collected on our tights.

But soon we'd warm, with hugs galore,
A group huddle, hearts to the core.
In winter's chill, we felt the glow,
Together we laughed, through ice and snow!

Markings on a Shimmering Surface

On glistening ground, a race begun,
Tripping over, oh! That was fun!
Each slip and slide, like a clumsy jig,
Our laughter rang, doing a funny gig.

Puddles froze, a skating spree,
With each misstep, a fit of glee.
We twirled and tumbled, hit the ground,
Then giggled loud, in joy we drowned.

Snowflakes laughing, tickling our cheeks,
In frosty air, we shared our weeks.
With every cheer, a memory made,
As winter wild, our spirits played.

All the slips, mishaps we wore,
Turned to tales to share, not bore.
In frosty fun, we found our bliss,
Each mark a memory, wrapped in a kiss!

Silhouettes in the Glacial Silence

Under a night sky, frosty stars,
We sketched our names on chilly jars.
With gleaming lights, we took to the scene,
Creating tales, like a silly dream.

Whispers of snowflakes, gentle and light,
We danced like shadows, oh what a sight!
Stomping and prancing, without a care,
While frost nipped at us with a frosty flare.

In icy corners, we made our mark,
Each giggle echoed, a fun little spark.
With frosty breath, we played our part,
And carved out fun, straight from the heart.

In glacial silence, joy we pursued,
With every chuckle, our spirits renewed.
As winter painted on its frosty slate,
We wrote our laughter, never too late!

Frosted Murmurs of Forgotten Steps

Tiny prints on icy ground,
Squeaky shoes, a giggling sound.
Bouncing, slipping, what a sight,
Winter's prank under moonlight.

Puffs of breath like dragon smoke,
Snowballs fly, a playful joke.
Laughter echoes, cold air thick,
Who knew that snow could be so slick?

Wobbly gaits and flailing arms,
Nature's dance with silly charms.
In this chill, we find delight,
While the world gleams, frosty white.

Memory trails marked by our cheer,
Each step forward, a chance to steer.
In the morning light, we can see,
Frosty laughter's legacy!

Essence of Walks by Firelight

S'mores sticky on frosty hands,
Outside laughter, wild and grand.
These winter walks, a merry spree,
Step on snow? Oh, plea-se don't flee!

Chasing shadows through the chill,
Sunset whispers, laughter's thrill.
Ghosts of joy in every flakes,
Watch out for pranks and silly jakes!

Around the fire, tales now grow,
Of those who fell in frosty glow.
With cocoa hugs, we share our fate,
Not all steps lead to snowy plates!

In warmth we bask, outside's a show,
With silly tales of walks in snow.
Each hearty laugh adds to this night,
Across the frost, our hearts feel light!

Icy Echos in the Stillness

In silence falls a soft white veil,
Echoes ring, as we set sail.
Icy paths with laughter weave,
Who can step, and then believe?

Crisp air bites, our noses red,
Every step a dance we tread.
Slips and giggles fill the air,
Nature's chuckle, a frigid dare!

Snowflakes swirl, a wild ride,
As we tumble, and there's no pride.
Each fall a splat, each rise a cheer,
Winter's humor brings us near!

In this white, we play and sing,
Joyful jests the winter brings.
With every slip and frosty twist,
We laugh until it's hard to resist!

Trails of Life Beneath the Snow

Beneath the blanket, secrets hide,
Footsteps dancing, come take a ride.
Wobbly paths that twist and turn,
In frozen laughter, we all learn.

Wanna race? But what a joke,
Snowballs fly, and then we croak!
Who knew we could fly so far?
Chasing joy beneath the star.

Winter's canvas, bright and wide,
Contraptions built, it's quite a ride.
Frosty wings and silly flights,
Creating magic on cold nights!

Who needs to warm by the fire's glow?
When we can dance in moonlit snow!
Each misstep makes us laugh and play,
In the chill, we find our way!

Cold Ventures and Warm Echoes

In the chill, a slip, a slide,
Watch the penguin dance with pride.
Snowflakes land on every nose,
As we laugh at winter's prose.

With every step, a crunching sound,
Fumbling feet on icy ground.
We twirl like leaves in winter's glee,
Two left feet, as happy as can be.

Socks and mittens lose their fight,
Frosty toes in sheer delight.
Hot cocoa waits, we race for cheer,
Tripping through the frozen sphere.

A snowball flies, a burst of white,
Laughter echoes, pure delight.
Oh, what fun in this freeze frame,
Cold adventures, always the same.

Tranquil Steps in the Winter Light

Beneath the pines, a frosty path,
With each slip, a cozy laugh.
Giggling friends on ice we tread,
Bouncing as we lose our stead.

Snowmen wink with carrot eyes,
While we find our merry ties.
Chasing shadows in the gleam,
Running wild, we ice-dream.

Twirling hats fly off our heads,
As we skip over snowy beds.
With each tumble, joy expands,
Winter magic in our hands.

In quiet steps, we seek the thrill,
Over hills and every chill.
Bolstered by the frigid fun,
Unraveled hearts, the day is won.

Sparkling Trails of a Quiet Stroll

Glistening paths beneath our feet,
Every step a chilly treat.
Joking how the ground does shake,
As we dance, we wiggle, quake.

Snowflakes twirl in jaunty flight,
Hats askew, what a funny sight.
Just like penguins, we parade,
In this winter, joy invades.

With frosty breath, we make our mark,
Imprints glowing in the dark.
A whispered giggle, shivering sighs,
Oh, how laughter never lies.

Slipping here, we spin and roll,
Each great fall, a happy goal.
Winter's laughter fills the air,
In our game, we have no care.

The Dance of the Winter Footfall

In this dance of frosted grace,
We trip and spin, a merry chase.
With every hop, our joy ignites,
As we dash into snowy nights.

Our cheeks aglow, like Rudolph's nose,
The chilly air, how it froze.
Stumbling through the snowy haze,
We share our laughs in winter's maze.

Catch a snowball on your chin,
Look at you, the fun begins!
Like graceful moose, we prance about,
Fallen snowflakes, stomp and shout.

In the frosty, biting air,
Every giggle, every flare.
Winter's charm, we can't reject,
For in this dance, we feel perfect.

Inscribed Memories on a Frosty Heart

On chilly days we dash and spin,
Our noses red, with grins so wide.
Each slip and slide, a playful sin,
Our frosty hearts can't hide.

With snowballs flying, laughter rings,
A snowman grins with a carrot nose.
We're quite the crew, oh what fun brings,
As winter's charm adds to our prose.

We trip and tumble, yet we cheer,
For every flake makes spirits bright.
In frozen air, our joy is clear,
While winter wraps us snug all night.

These memories carved in icy glaze,
Encountered laughter, all around.
Through swirling winds, in winter's maze,
We find our bliss, so joyfully bound.

The Journey of Cold Breaths

With every breath, a frosty puff,
We march like penguins, silly and proud.
Chasing snowflakes, oh what a bluff,
We stumble, crash, and laugh out loud.

The icicles hang like toothy grins,
A comical sight from the trees above.
We skate and slide, with cheeky spins,
Embracing winter, as wrapped in love.

Hot cocoa spills, the mugs all laugh,
While mittens glide on frosty curls.
We make our way like silly giraffes,
Through swirling snow and whirling twirls.

Yet as we tread on nature's floor,
We leave a tale of quirky glee.
These chilly times, we can't ignore,
Forever etched in memory.

Layers of Time in Snowy Traces

In a soft blanket, the world is new,
We dash through snow with childlike grace.
A wiggle here, a frosty chew,
As laughter paints a smiling face.

Each layer thick with stories shared,
Banana peels, and slips galore.
Frosty highs where no one dared,
As winter whispers, "Just explore!"

The gingerbread men all lose their heads,
As we compete in snowy races.
Funny memories while we tread,
In nature's quilt of bright white laces.

With every slide, our spirits thrive,
Creating joys in winter's grasp.
For in this chill, we feel alive,
Each memory slips away, we clasp.

Wading through Winter's Embrace

A waddle here, a dance of glee,
As flakes cascade like jokes on air.
With flurry and cheer, we set it free,
Into the cold, we leap without care.

The wind it howls, a prankster's delight,
Our hats fly off as we chase the storm.
Through snowy paths, we giggle tight,
Adventures shared, all cozy and warm.

Snowmen wobble, their sticks in place,
Accidental tumbling—oh, what a sight!
With carrot noses and frosty grace,
Our winter whimsy takes its flight.

So here we roam, in laughter's grasp,
Through fuzzy mitts and chilly air.
With every silly joke, we clasp,
These moments bright beyond compare.

Whispers Beneath the Ice

The squirrels are plotting, it's quite a sight,
In snowman hats, they dance in delight.
Their tiny paws leave patterns so bold,
As they gather acorns, the secrets unfold.

A penguin in boots, he wobbles with flair,
On slippery patches, he tumbles through air.
Laughing, the owls hoot, what a grand show,
When winter reveals its playful tableau.

The rabbits are racing, with snowballs to toss,
In a fluffy white world, they seem quite the boss.
Chasing their shadows, they leap and they bound,
In a frosty arena, hilarity's found.

At twilight, the snowflakes start making a scene,
Collecting in piles like fluff on a bean.
With giggles and snickers, they twirl in the air,
Whispers of laughter that travel with care.

Traces in the Snowlight

The frost-bitten critters all frolic and squeak,
In a snowball battle, they clash for a week.
Fluffy-tailed comrades, so proud and so spry,
Snowflakes fall gently, and so do they fly.

A sneaky old badger with mischief to spread,
Puts on his best scarf and tips back his head.
He dives into snowdrifts, his laughter resounds,
With each snowy splat, pure joy knows no bounds.

A trio of mice in a cabaret show,
Dance on their toes, put quite the high-low.
With acrobatic flips, they cause quite the thrill,
While birds stop to watch, they can't get their fill.

As stars start to twinkle, the sun takes its rest,
Snowmen take tips from a circusing jest.
Their carrot-nosed grins, wide and full of cheer,
Sprinkle the night with laughter so clear.

Echoes of Winter's Breath

The trees in their jackets are shaking in glee,
As snowflakes fall off like confetti from a spree.
The squirrels throw parties, and who could resist?
When winter plays tricks, it tops the list!

A fidgety fox with a coat made of fluff,
Tries to outsmart a snowdrift, just too tough.
He tumbles and rolls in a rather fine style,
And the hares all giggle, oh isn't that wild?

The snowmen gossip in hats far too tall,
About the funny shapes they see on the wall.
With noses of carrots and eyes made of coal,
They recount their adventures while losing control.

As night falls upon them, the fun never ends,
With snowflakes like dancers, they sway with their friends.
Through whispers of laughter, the echoes arise,
In this whimsical winter, where joy never dies.

Silent Steps on Crystal Paths

The shadows of snowbirds play peek-a-boo games,
While bears in their mittens declare silly claims.
With frosty moustaches that twirl and that spin,
They march through the winter, a humorous din.

A lone little penguin walks fancily there,
Wearing mismatched socks — oh, what a rare pair!
With jazz in his stride, he glides past the crowd,
As chuckles abound, they cheer, "You're so proud!"

The snowflakes giggle as they swirl and drift,
Touching on rooftops, now this is their gift.
And puppies leap joyfully, paws flying fast,
Creating a ballet of blunders that last.

In moonlight, the bunny starts leading a dance,
With a jig and a hop, it's a holiday chance.
Their laughter rings bright through the crisp winter air,
A merry ensemble, with love to spare.

Stillness Captured in Crystal Trails

Paws in the snow, a waddle so bold,
Belly-flops sliding, never gets old.
Squirrels are giggling, they scatter and soar,
While I'm stuck laughing, falling once more.

Icicles dangle, they glimmer and gleam,
Whispers of winter, a frosty daydream.
I'll chase down the penguins with penguin-like flair,
But slip on a patch and fly through the air.

Cuddled in mittens, I'm fluffed like a bear,
Snowflakes like confetti, landing everywhere.
My scarf's all twisted, a fashion faux pas,
Yet, who can resist a snowball bazaar?

With each frozen step, I giggle and grin,
As frostbite singing, it's calling me in.
Laughs echo softly, while snowflakes descend,
In this crystal ballet, my clumsy best friend.

Unseen Journeys on the Chilled Horizon

A snowman wobbles, his buttons askew,
His carrot nose quivers, 'what should I do?'
He calls out to snowflakes, "Let's have some fun!"
But gets buried under an avalanche run.

The birds at the feeder, they squawk and they shout,
As I set a trap to sneakily scout.
Their dance in the air, so fluffy and bright,
But I'm stuck in the snow, just losing the fight.

With mittens on hands, I feel like a clown,
My whole body tumbles, I twist and I frown.
I try to look graceful, a ballerina vibe,
But I'm just a snowfish, flopping and bribe.

And when I look back, what chaos I've made,
A trail full of giggles, a leisurely parade.
This winter wilderness, so frosty, so dear,
Is better when shared with a chuckle and cheer.

Warmth Shimmering Beneath the Cold

Under layers of wool, I dance with delight,
Hot cocoa in hand, it feels cozy and right.
Outside it is chilly, but I'm feeling grand,
While my toes are still thawing from snow's icy hand.

The firewood's popping, the marshmallows roast,
I make a sweet s'more, now that is the most.
My friends in the cabin, they laugh and they tease,
As I drop my last bite, a chocolatey sneeze!

We dream of the summer, the sunshine's embrace,
Yet every clumsy moment, I welcome with grace.
For beneath the ice-cold, there's warmth in the fun,
And laughter resounds 'til the day's finally done.

So here is to winter, with its chilly air,
Where giggles and snowflakes are scattered with care.
In this playground of frost, we'll laugh and we'll play,
'Cause nothing beats warmth, on a cold winter's day.

Traces That Tell a Timeless Tale

In boots made for dancing, I leap and I glide,
I'll twirl on the surface, see how I can ride.
But under my feet, it's a slippery grace,
As I spin like a top and collide face-to-face!

A squirrel and I, we'd have a great chat,
He stops and he stares, with a flick of his hat.
"Do watch for that patch!" he chirps with delight,
But I'm busy inventing a snow angel flight.

Downhill with laughter, I race through the trees,
But the path takes a twist, oh what a tease!
My sled takes a detour, straight down to the creek,
I emerge like a seal—what a rosy red cheek!

Yet every mishap's a treasure, you see,
Like stories told warm by the crackling spree.
In dreaming of summers, we still dance with cheer,
To the rhythms of winter, my friends gather near.

White Canopy of Uncharted Hearts

In the fluff, we dance with glee,
Wobbling like penguins, can't you see?
Face-planting here, a laugh we share,
Fluffy white clouds in the chilly air.

Sledding down with all our might,
Snowballs flying, oh what a sight!
Faces aglow, we play on repeat,
Winter's a party, now isn't that sweet?

The snowman's head rolls off with a thud,
We giggle and slip in the cold, wet mud.
With scarves that spin like wild kite tails,
We're grand adventurers, leaving funny trails.

Each flake that falls is its own wisecrack,
As we stumble and giggle, there's never a lack.
So come join the fun, lose your winter blues,
In this white wonderland, there's laughter to choose!

Quiet Harmonies of Frozen Paths

Walking on ice, we prance with flair,
A slip here and there—oh, beware!
An orchestra of giggles fills the air,
As we glide like graceful bears in a chair.

With tiny boots, we create a symphony,
A waltz of blunders, oh so carefree!
The cold wind whispers, 'Try not to fall,'
But we take a tumble, and giggles enthrall.

Hot cocoa dreams in the frosty glow,
Our cheeks are rosy—it's all quite a show!
Snowflakes sprinkle our hair like confetti,
While we dance on the ice, oh so unsteady.

The sun sets low, painting skies of pink,
We plop on the snow, take a moment to think.
Winter's charm makes us feel anew,
With laughter and snow, it's a joyous view!

Paths of Memories in the Glaze

On the ice, we slide and schmooze,
With tipsy twirls in our winter shoes.
A slippery dance, we seem to not care,
As laughter erupts from each frosty glare.

Family portraits all come alive,
With snowball fights that help us thrive.
Our hats askew, a sight to behold,
In this chilly weather, our fun is bold.

Remember that time we all took a leap?
And landed in piles, giggling heaps!
Those moments freeze, like the winter air,
Encased in laughter, beyond compare.

With chilly friends and rosy cheeks,
We create memories and little 'squeaks.'
In frozen realms where joy takes its place,
We dance on the ice—what a silly race!

Beyond the Chill of the Winding Way

It starts with a chill, then warms to delight,
As we bundle up snug beneath the bright light.
Hot cocoa runs, oh how we compete,
To produce the best, it's a wondrous feat.

Snowball diplomacy, we form our own peace,
In creative mayhem, our laughter won't cease.
Chasing our shadows, we tumble and roll,
With winter as canvas, together we stroll.

The trees stand tall, cloaked in white shrouds,
We caper beneath them, oh how they're proud!
Each step crunches loud, a symphony plays,
As we navigate pathways where fun never strays.

So here's to the cold and the laughter it brings,
To snow-covered mornings and all that it sings.
In this frosty wonderland, friendship stays tight,
As we soar through the chill, hearts warm with delight!

Beneath the Frigid Veil

In winter's chill, I slipped and fell,
A dance with snow, oh what a spell!
The ground's a prankster, ice so sly,
Made me twirl like I could fly.

With every step, a giggle here,
As neighbors watch, they give a cheer.
A frosty ballet, but no applause,
Just snowflakes clapping with cold claws.

I tried to prance like Bambi, bold,
But ended up with limbs ice-cold.
My dog just laughed, what a delight,
In this frosty world, a clumsy sight.

So under this coat of winter white,
I'll jig and jive; it's pure delight.
Each slip, a laugh, a tale to share,
Beneath this chill, I have no care.

Hush of Winter's Footfalls

In winter's hush, I made a scene,
My snowman friend, a wobble routine.
With carrot nose and arms askew,
He giggled as I stumbled too.

With every crunch beneath my shoe,
I heard the snowflakes whisper, 'Boo!'
Is that a footprint? Oh, it's a game,
An icy horse, not quite the same.

And as I slipped on icy ground,
A squirrel laughed, what a silly sound!
It scurried past on tiny paws,
While I just sprawled with frozen jaws.

So here's to winter, full of jest,
With frosty air, I'm truly blessed.
Each fall, each slip, a comic note,
In this snowy tale, I'll gloat.

Cold Silhouettes at Dusk

As dusk descends, shadows play,
I pranced outside, my feet a ballet.
The ground so slick, my graceful try,
Ended with me, a snowman sigh.

The icicles glinted, such a sight,
While I tripped over, left and right.
The trees stood tall, in silent cheer,
As I narrated my frosty fear.

I chuckled loud, my face went red,
A jig on ice, a wobbly spread.
Cold silhouettes, dancing around,
While laughter echoed, a joyful sound.

So here's my tale of winter's dance,
With frosty giggles, I took a chance.
In every slip, a story made,
In this crisp air, my humor played.

Journey through the Whispering Frost

In a whispering world of chilly cheer,
I ventured forth with clumsy gear.
The snowflakes teased, 'Let's have some fun!'
As I bounced by, my shoes weighed a ton.

With giggles near, my dog took flight,
Through snowdrifts deep, a comical sight.
We raced and rolled, a frosty spree,
But ended up stuck under a tree.

As I flopped down, breathless and bright,
I spotted a snowman grinning in spite.
He waved his stick arms, all dressed in white,
While I lay there, in pure delight.

So here's my journey, through frosty trails,
With laughter loud, as winter wails.
Each slip, a joy, each fall, a roar,
In the frosty world, who could ask for more?

The Memory of Steps on Ice

They slipped and slid, oh what a scene,
A ballet on ice, a comical routine.
With arms outstretched, they tried to glide,
But fell on their backs, laughing wide.

With each brave step, their courage bold,
Like penguins they waddled, out in the cold.
One twirled and spun, like a dervish on snow,
While others just aimed for the nearest warm glow.

A snowman watched, with a grin on his face,
As they slipped and tumbled, all over the place.
Each icy fall met with giggles and cheers,
Creating a patchwork of joyful sneers.

The memory lingers, a giggly delight,
As they reminisce those cold, frosty nights.
For every misstep, a story to tell,
Of laughter and warmth, where all friends fell.

Solace Found on Icy Journeys

They trekked out on ice with grand hopes in tow,
But one missed a step, and oh, what a show!
Like a deer on a slide, they flailed through the air,
Landing face-first, for a snow-capped affair.

Hot cocoa dreams danced in their minds,
As their mates rolled on laughing, one nearly blinds.
With snowballs a-throwing, they geared up for fun,
Who knew winter mischief could brighten the sun?

They formed goofy chains, of slips and of falls,
With a chorus of chuckles, echoing calls.
Each frostbitten slip turned to joyous glee,
Uniting them all in sheer comedy.

Through icy adventures, they found little bliss,
In laughter and warmth, they couldn't resist.
With each frozen moment turned playful and bright,
They'll remember those trips until summer's light.

Echoes on the Icy Path

Along the path where the chill winds play,
Echoes of laughter chase worries away.
A slip, then a tumble, a cascade of squeals,
As the icy grip shows just how it feels.

One spins like a top, another ducks low,
And a tumbleweed's dance steals the show.
They forge on ahead, though their shoes betray,
With each little slip, they just laugh and sway.

The ice crackles sweetly, as if in on the jest,
Each fall like applause, they think they are blessed.
With raucous delight, the whole crew's in cheer,
Every stumble a victory, each slip brings a tear!

At dusk they will gather, with cups made of cheer,
To relive the chaos that lightened their year.
While frosty misfortune tried hard to win,
The echoes of joy turned the loss into grin.

Whispers Beneath the Snow

Through whispering snow where the shadows play,
They bundled up tight and slid all the way.
Oh but the ice held its secrets in bounds,
As each tiny slip turned to wild, laughter sounds.

Beware of the ice, the friends all declared,
But that didn't stop them; they skated and dared.
One slipped on a patch, did a dance in the air,
While the rest fell like dominoes, without a care.

The cold air erupted with giggles and shouts,
As snowballs took flight, amidst joyful round bouts.
They reveled in winter, their spirits so bright,
With snowmen for company on this frosty night.

Underneath all the snow, whispers of fun,
Of friendships that warm like the welcoming sun.
A symphony played in the chill of the air,
For laughter is best when you're all in the bare.

Frosted Dreams of Heartfelt Journeys

In the morning chill, I slip and slide,
Beneath my feet, the ice did hide.
I dance like a penguin, what a sight!
Winter's ballet, oh, what pure delight!

Snowflakes fall, a ticklish cheer,
Each one whispers, 'Winter's here!'
With cheeks aglow, I trip and grin,
In my frosty dreams, let the fun begin!

Around the corner, a snowball flies,
A friendly fight with frosty sighs.
Laughter echoes through the white,
As snowmen dance into the night.

So let us frolic, through snow and ice,
In each stumble, there's sweet surprise.
With every slip, there's joy anew,
In the winter wonderland, just us two!

Murmurs of Nature in the Cold

The trees wear coats of shimmering white,
Chitchat in whispers of pure delight.
Squirrels scamper with nuts in tow,
While penguins march, saying 'Don't be slow!'

Icicles dangle, aiming for fun,
Dripping like laughter from warm winter sun.
A snowman grins with a carrot nose,
'You'll never guess how cold it goes!'

When snowflakes twirl in the frosty breeze,
Nature giggles among the trees.
They conspire to tickle your toes,
In this winter realm where humor flows.

So come, take a stroll, it's a wild ride,
With chilly antics to turn the tide.
With frosty humor, you'll soon see,
Winter's a jester, with joy as the key!

Crystal Impressions in Twilight

Under the stars, in a glistening glow,
Last night's antics begin to show.
Bunny hops leaving traces so bright,
As I chuckle at their frosty flight.

With every step on the icy ground,
A symphony of crunching sounds.
Elves on sleds race by in glee,
While I waddle, a sight to see!

Winter's mischief is on full display,
A snowball battle, come what may!
Cheeks like apples, rosy and round,
In this chilly embrace, laughter's found.

So grab your hat, come join the fun,
As we dance under the wintry sun.
With every giggle, we make our mark,
In nature's playground, from dawn till dark!

Cascades of Winter's Whispering

In a world where the cold whispers play,
I trip on ice, with grace gone astray.
Snowflakes giggle as they softly fall,
While I tumble in joy, a winter ball!

The snowmen's grin stretches ear to ear,
Waving hello, they spread winter cheer.
'Careful now,' they seem to chime,
'Falling's the best, just look at our time!'

A frosty breeze teases my hat,
While icicles dangle, oh, where are they at?
Nature's humor sparkles and shines,
As I slip and slide on these frosty lines.

So gather your friends and let's create,
A joyous scene, the best kind of fate.
In this glad winter, laughter ignites,
With every flurry, our hearts take flight!

Moments Frozen in Time

In the morning chill, I pranced so bold,
Chasing after snowflakes, twirling like gold.
But my boots betrayed me, a slip and a slide,
Down to the ground, oh what a ride!

Laughter erupted from trees all around,
As I made snow angels, flopping, profound.
Then my dog jumped in, with a splash of delight,
Turning my bliss into a frosty fight!

With frosty eyebrows, I rose from the snow,
My face like a tomato, shining aglow.
"Look at this mess!" I chuckled, bemused,
Life's frozen moments, so silly, so used!

Yet every misstep, I wore like a crown,
In this winter wonder, I laughed and I frowned.
Tomorrow, the world will be fresh with white cheer,
But today, I'll treasure the fun that's right here!

Shimmering Traces of a Story Untold

A waltz in the snow, my steps in a flurry,
With shimmy and shuffle, oh what a hurry!
Then I slipped on a patch that was slick as a seal,
The ice claimed my dignity, what a big deal!

My neighbor observed from behind a warm curtain,
Trying to stifle laughter, the tension was certain.
When I rolled like a log, 'twas quite the display,
"I'll get you hot cocoa!" I shouted in play.

The prints that I left told a tale, a tad wild,
Of a dancer whose rhythm was thoroughly riled.
Each step made a pattern, a jigsaw of fun,
For every mischance, there's laughter to be won!

And as I regained my composure with flair,
The snow looked so inviting, no longer a scare.
Next time I'll waltz with a little more grace,
But until then, I'll embrace the silliness in space!

Silent Whisper of the Frozen Earth

The plumes of my breath, like tiny white puffs,
Echoed my giggles, as winter got rough.
There's a secret in snow, it's soft, it's so sly,
You can tumble and roll, but no one knows why!

A dance near the trees, I felt so enchanted,
Till my boots caught the edge and my balance was chanted.
Down went my backside, right into the heap,
Of frosty white pillows, which made me lose sleep.

Majestic was my fall, a sight to behold,
The snow, like my audience, a throne made of gold.
But as I lay giggling, the sun passed me by,
Leaving me chortling with an inch to comply!

So I gathered my pride, in my tangled up clothes,
And left little stories in the shape of my toes.
For winter can be a whimsical foe,
With laughter as armor, just go with the flow!

The Subtle Art of Leaving Marks

I ventured outside where the snow was so thick,
Each step was a gamble, oh what a slick trick!
With enthusiasm high, and my scarf tied just right,
I danced like a penguin, a curious sight!

But oh, there was trouble beneath every flair,
A patch of black ice, like a hidden snare.
I tiptoed so slow, then boom! I was gone,
Like a cartoonish figure, slipping toward dawn.

The laughter of kids rang like bells in the air,
As I landed with flair, without any care.
In snowflakes and giggles, we'd weave tales unspun,
Creating the magic of wintertime fun!

So on with the capers, the tumble and chase,
With every misstep, a smile on my face.
For in life's crazy moments, it's joy that we trace,
Each mark in the snow tells a tale of our grace!

Frost-Kissed Remembrance

In a hurry, I tripped, oh dear,
My coffee spilled, worse than a smear.
I dance on ice, with quite the flair,
A winter waltz, without a care.

Each step I take, a giggle breaks,
Slipping here, as my balance shakes.
Cursing at socks that feel too tight,
The snowman laughs; I'm quite the sight!

Snowflakes swirl like confetti, hooray!
I build a snowman, a chilly ballet.
But as I turn, I feel a sprain,
It seems my dance has caused some pain!

Yet with each fall, I rise with glee,
For laughter's warmth is all I need.
I'll waddle home, a sight to see,
With frosty hair and frozen knee!

The Silent Journey in White

Crunch of snow beneath my feet,
A bumpy ride, oh what a feat!
My cat runs past, in a furry blur,
I chase behind, like quite the cur!

An igloo formed, my regal throne,
Yet every king's fate is well-known.
A pitfall found, I take a dive,
Beneath the snow, I barely survive!

Each twist and turn, a snowy prank,
The winter's humor—never blank.
I shovel paths, then lose my grip,
And down I go, a silly slip!

But with laughter bright, I rise and shout,
For winter's fun is what it's about.
So let those gales bring icy cheer,
I'll sing aloud, with no fear here!

Lace of Ice Beneath the Pines

Sprinkled lace on branches high,
I shuffle past, a wondering sigh.
But tripped on air, oh clumsy me,
The trees now laugh; they're wild with glee.

A bird flies by, and gives a quirk,
While I'm down here, doing my work.
My gloves now soaked, my socks are wet,
I wonder if my fall's a threat!

Snow angels made from flailing arms,
Not the graceful kind—oh, such charms!
The pines stand proud as I'm sprawled wide,
Their laughter echoes, none can hide.

But up I spring with snowy flair,
With giggles bright, I comb my hair.
For in this chill, with every slip,
I find sweet joy in winter's grip!

Slices of Life on the Blanket

A blanket white, so fresh and clean,
But watch your step—oh, what a scene!
I tried to leap, a joyful bound,
But landed face down; the snow's profound.

The dog runs wild, a furry blur,
As I chase him, oh what a stir!
A tumble here, a roll down there,
We end up tangled in frosty air.

With snowball fights that turn to fun,
I duck and dodge under the sun.
But oh, surprise! A snowball flies,
And all I see are blurry skies!

But winter's cheer won't let me frown,
With each cold fall, I turn around.
For laughter blooms in snow so bright,
And every slip is pure delight!

Imprints of Wanderers at Dawn

Dawn breaks with giggles and grins,
A dance in the chilly air begins.
Tiny footprints trail in a zigzag,
Squeaky boots, oh what a snag!

Snowball fights spark rule-bending,
An icy mess, but no one's ending.
Sliding down hills, a wobbly race,
With laughter echoing, we embrace.

Forgotten mittens, lost in the blight,
A quest for warmth in the morning light.
With each frosty slip and a slip 'n' slide,
Winter mischief, we take in stride!

A snowy patch, a canvas wide,
A snowman's hat, a wobbly guide.
We leave our marks, we leave our cheer,
In this goofy, frosty frontier!

Signatures on a Snowy Dream

In the hush of white ground, we play,
With sleds that zip and gleeful sway.
Our giggles carve the frosty air,
As we tumble, fall, and lose our hair!

Snowflakes tumble, we flail and spin,
Chasing each other, double the grin.
With every roll, we leave a print,
The best kind of mess, a snowman's hint.

Hats upside down and scarves askew,
Who needs rules? We'll make do!
Boots full of snow, "Oh what a sight!"
You've got to love this frosty delight!

Our snowy dreams written so bright,
A canvas of laughter in the cold light.
Tomorrow will come, and so will the sun,
But for now, the winter's just begun!

Chill of the Wandering Soul

A shiver runs through every bone,
In this winter realm, we roam alone.
With hot cocoa and snazzy hats,
We'll embrace the chill, just like chitchats!

Frosty cheeks and slippery shows,
The chilly dance is how it goes.
Stumbling about in a laughing spree,
Each fall's a show, come watch me, see!

We leave a trail of glee behind,
With every skip, so unrefined.
Snowmen come alive, with carrot noses,
As we frolic where the cold wind blows us!

So here we are, the wandering crew,
Strutting our stuff in a world of blue.
Frozen giggles, what a grand role,
In this icy jam, we find our soul!

Beneath the Frosted Veil

Under a blanket, so frosty and white,
We march like kids, full of delight.
With each little step, a giggle's born,
In this winter tale, where we are sworn!

Snowball warfare and curious pets,
In this frosted world, we have no regrets.
A slip and a slide, we dart with cheer,
And every stumble brings us near!

Our jackets puffed like marshmallows round,
A wintery fashion we've proudly found.
With laughter echoes, we leap and bound,
Having the time of our lives, profound!

So let's leave our marks in icy delight,
Beneath the veil of winter's might.
Funny moments, forever unfold,
In this frosty kingdom, we will be bold!

The Glimmering Dance of Snowflakes

Snowflakes swirl in a jolly parade,
Dancing with glee, their frosty charade.
They tickle my nose, a cold little tease,
As I slip on the ice, oh, where are my keys?

The air's full of laughter, like kids on a spree,
Each flake a performer in winter's grand spree.
I try to catch one, it vanishes quick,
Right on my tongue, it melts like a trick!

Hot cocoa awaits after snowball fights,
With marshmallows bobbing like fluffy white bites.
We giggle and chuckle, our cheeks rosy bright,
As snowflakes keep twirling, what a whimsical sight!

Embrace the cold chaos, let joy cascade,
With snowmen and angels, a frosty parade.
So when winter visits, let's seize every chance,
To frolic and tumble in snow's silly dance!

Sweet Echoes of Winter's Heart

Winter whispers softly, a playful refrain,
Pulling us closer with giggles and pain.
Slippers on ice, a ballet gone wrong,
With slips and with trips, we'll laugh all day long.

Chilly winds blow as we bundle up tight,
Mittens are missing, oh what a sight!
Snowflakes are dancing, with mischief in tow,
I'll dodge all the flurries, just you watch me go!

Hot pancakes for breakfast, syrup on my face,
Turning my kitchen into a sticky race.
Each bite is a giggle, joy stacked up high,
While snowmen outside toss snowballs in the sky!

The season keeps chuckling, hiding its spree,
With snowball ambushes and tumbling glee.
So bring on the frost, with its chilly embrace,
Let's dance with the winter, a heartwarming chase!

The Hidden Stories Beneath the Surface

Footprints trace tales where secrets are spun,
In smooth white blankets where snowflakes have fun.
A rabbit, a squirrel, they dodge and they weave,
While I attempt skiing, I won't dare to leave!

I find a lost mitten, a hat in a tree,
What stories they tell, of laughter and glee.
A snowball's sharp humor, it flies through the air,
Only to hit—oh dear, wait, was that my hair?

Underneath snowdrifts, there's mischief galore,
With hidden adventures, and giggles in store.
Each layer a chapter, from silly to bright,
As winter unfolds with a sparkling light.

So gather your friends, and let stories unfold,
In this canvas of white, let laughter be bold.
Embrace every flurry, the joy that's our guide,
With memories sparkling, like snowflakes, we'll glide!

Chills of Change Across the Landscape

The landscape's transforming, a chilly delight,
With nature's own brush, it paints day and night.
Icicles giggle, like teeth of a grin,
As I slip down the hill, my sledding begins.

Frosty air tickles, it bites at our nose,
While snowmen stand guard, in their wintery clothes.
We sketch out our laughter in the snow's frozen art,
Oh, winter, you tricky, you warm my cold heart!

With each flake that lands, it brings tales anew,
From snowball fights played to hot soup for two.
A dog in a sweater does zoomies nearby,
While I try to outrun icy tracks with a sigh.

As the sun meets the snow, watch the sparkle ignite,
The world fades away in this frosty delight.
So grab your scarves tight, let's embrace this wild fate,
For winter's sweet secrets are never too late!

Murmurs in the Icy Air

In the crispness, we doth tread,
As squirrels giggle overhead.
With each crunch underfoot, we find,
The snowman grinning, unconfined.

Muffled laughter, slipping fast,
A winter dance, a snowy blast.
With rosy cheeks, we take a spin,
Who knew cold could bring such grins?

Chasing snowflakes, wildly near,
Beware the ice, oh dear, oh dear!
A little tumble, giggles bright,
We're kings and queens of snowy heights.

So let's embrace this frosty cheer,
With frosty puns that we hold dear.
In the chill, we'll make our mark,
As laughter and fun ignite the spark.

Secrets Beneath the Snow's Embrace

Under blankets white and soft,
A secret squirrel darts aloft.
Whispers hide beneath the veil,
Of mischief and a snowy trail.

Penguins wobble, quite a sight,
In winter gear, oh what a fright!
Snowflakes tickle noses bare,
As snowmen grumble, 'Life's not fair!'

Ice slides slyly, hearts feel bold,
Adventures in the winter cold.
Snowball fights and winter's jest,
Only the brave will find true zest.

With every crunch, a tale unfolds,
Of frozen secrets, laughter holds.
So gather 'round, let's share a joke,
While warming up beside the smoke.

Chilling Imprints in Serenity

In quiet fields where silence reigns,
We tiptoe lightly, making gains.
With playful hearts and chilly toes,
We create a scene, how it glows!

A friendly pup comes bounding near,
With frosty breath, no hint of fear.
He leaps in snow with joyful flair,
While we chuckle at his airborne hair.

Snowball packing, eyes aglow,
Watch out, friend! Here it comes, oh no!
A hit, a laugh, it zips right past,
Maybe next time, but never last!

So we dance through this winter dream,
Beneath the sun's bright, gleaming beam.
In this chill, we'll keep it light,
With laughter echoing, pure delight.

Waking Dreams on a Frozen Trail

As morning dawns, the world's aglow,
We stroll the path where snowflakes flow.
Eyes wide open, eager as can be,
We trip and tumble, oh, look at me!

Shovels clash while people grumble,
Yet in this mess, we laugh and tumble.
Snowmen rise with hats too big,
While snowballs fly with a wild jig.

And out of nowhere, here comes the cat,
Slipping and sliding, imagine that!
Chasing shadows on this frigid lane,
While laughter bubbles like warm champagne.

So here's to fun on winter's stage,
In playful moments, we engage.
With frosty humor, we'll prevail,
As stories weave along the trail.

Eternal Tracks on Shrouded Ground

In winter's chill, my feet did slide,
I zigzagged wide, a frosty ride.
Chasing squirrels who just stared back,
With every slip, I lost my track.

A dance of grace, a frosty jig,
The neighbors laugh, their faces big.
Do they know that I'm the ice king?
Or just an elf with a broken wing?

The Poetry of Ice beneath Footfalls

Each step I take, the ice does creak,
Like a wise old man, it starts to speak.
"Beware, dear friend, of hidden slick!"
But I just laugh, and do a trick.

Oh what a sight, as I take flight,
One moment brave, the next in fright.
With flailing arms, I twist and flop,
My graceful moves? A total flop!

Frozen Murmurs on a Misty Morning

The morning mist, a ghostly shroud,
As I step out, feeling mighty proud.
But oh, the ground, it does conspire,
To send me flying, I could retire!

Like cartoons, I spin, I glide,
With every slip, my joy can't hide.
Laughter echoes through the trees,
At my ballet on the frozen freeze!

Breathing Life into Ice's Page

In winter's book, I leave my mark,
Drawn by laughter, near the park.
As I stumble, my pride does sway,
Rolling like dough, in a frosty play.

Each slip and trip, a story told,
Of epic fails, both brave and bold.
So if you spot me, give a cheer,
For laughter's the treasure of winter's sphere!

Impressions in the Chilling Dawn

In the biting chill of morning light,
Cats dance like they're on a tightrope,
While the snowmen wobble, what a sight,
As I trip over my frozen shoelace rope.

Snowflakes twirl like dizzy sprites,
While I try to find my mittens' pair,
Each step I take brings frosty bites,
My nose turns red, I swear it's not fair!

A squirrel snickers from a nearby tree,
As I slip in style, oh what a show!
He must think that it's funny to see,
My winter ballet, complete with a blow!

With winter's chill, I must concede,
That laughter keeps me warm inside,
In this frosty realm, I'll proceed,
Grinning wide as I clumsily glide.

Shadows of Solitude in Cold

In shadows cast by winter's might,
Trees stand like guardians of the day,
Huddled in coats, avoiding the bite,
While my breath forms clouds, drifting away.

An icicle dangles from the eave,
Like a stalactite, trying to tease,
But it's the penguin sweeping the leaves,
That really makes me weak in the knees!

I laugh as I face the frosty brunt,
Making angels with a floppy style,
Then a dog joins in on my hilarious stunt,
Rolling 'round, he spins with a smile.

With every step, the echoes call,
As laughter fills the quiet expanse,
In this solitude, we all have a ball,
Sharing giggles in our icy dance.

Canvas of Winter's Secrets

A canvas painted with powder so bright,
I tackle my walk like a stylish fall,
Each flake a secret, a delight,
While falling, I consider this a ball!

The trees are frosted, that's no lie,
Making shapes that seem to grin,
With an owl laughing from nearby,
It's obvious, he's ready to have a spin!

My boots make sounds like popcorn popping,
Each step's a chance to trip and land,
And as I tumble, not stopping,
The squirrels clap, you'd think it was planned!

In this white wonder, there's much to explore,
While giggles echo in the arctic air,
Winter's canvas is hard to ignore,
Painting smiles with each icy flair.

Signs of the Silent Season

In a world that glimmers with a chilly cheer,
Footprints say things like 'oops, oh no!'
I swear the snowflakes giggle, it's clear,
When I tumble, and serve them the show!

An icy patch calls me like a friend,
With a wink that says 'come slide right here,'
I meet the ground, it's a graceful end,
While snowballs aim to bust my veneer!

Those trees, they whisper secrets at night,
While I race past in a jingle-jangle,
Each branch swaying, in delight,
Making me feel like I should dangle!

This silent season, so deceptively sly,
Crafts laughter from every stumble and lead,
With winter's grin reflecting the sky,
If only my balance would match my speed!

Treads on the Crust of Time

In winter's chill, I take a stride,
My boots, they squeak, they slip, they slide.
The snowflakes dance, oh what a show,
Each step's a gamble—will I go slow?

With every slip, I spin and twirl,
My limbs flail out in an awkward whirl.
Grinning faces catch my fall,
I laugh it off like it's no big deal at all.

The neighbors giggle from their warm abode,
As I attempt to brave the frozen road.
A marble statue, I pose with flair,
Only to tumble with a frosty glare!

But through the laughter, cold bites my nose,
With icy puddles, I'll dodge, I'll doze.
Each slip a memory, a tale to share,
In the winter wonderland, I've stripped down to bare!

The Frosty Symphony of Solitude

In silence deep, the frost begins to play,
A symphony of shivers on display.
The trees, they shudder; the wind sings loud,
As I waltz alone in a misty shroud.

A rogue snowflake lands upon my brow,
I sneeze and snort—it's time to take a vow.
To be the king of this icy ballet,
But oh, how I trip and sway away!

The icicles hang like sharpened spears,
I dodge and weave, battling frozen fears.
Yet laughter bubbles from my frozen lips,
As I pirouette past snow-covered strips.

A lonely concert in a winter's night,
With frosty echoes and twinkling light.
And though I falter in this dance so grand,
I grin and giggle, a snow-dusted band!

Hunting for Warmth in Winter's Grasp

In search of warmth, I roam the block,
Shivering 'neath a woolly sock.
The heater's broken, the kettle's cold,
With every breath, I challenge the bold.

Through snowdrifts deep, I march ahead,
A brave explorer in winter's bed.
But alas! My quest, an uphill race,
I waddle like a penguin, a comical case!

Toasty dreams of cocoa dance in my mind,
While snowball fights leave laughter behind.
But frozen fingers try to hold the cup,
In a twist of fate, the hot drink goes up!

I'm destined for chaos on this chilly spree,
With every step, I pose as the winter's marquee.
Yet in this shiver, my spirit finds glee,
For hunting warmth is a fun jubilee!

Veils of Ice and Memories Night

Beneath a veil of icy lace,
I stomp around with a silly grace.
Every crunch sends echoes high,
As stars peek out from a frosty sky.

The air is sharp; my cheeks turn red,
With wobbly feet, I forge ahead.
And oh! A slip! I'm on the floor,
Rolling like a snowball, who could ask for more?

Memories sprout like snowflakes near,
Each laugh, each fall, I hold so dear.
A night of giggles, a slip 'n slide,
In the icy shrouds, my joy won't hide.

With veils of winter around me spun,
I stumble, trip, yet still have fun.
As laughter rings where the cold winds blow,
My heart is warm in the afterglow!